I
DREAM
OF
AFRICA

Poetry of Post-Independence Africa, the Case of Zambia

CHARLES MWEWA

ACP PRESS

2023

Published by:

AFRICA IN CANADA PRESS
Ottawa, Canada
www.acpress.ca

First published in 2015 as:
Sail without Ship

Reprinted with modification in 2023 as:
I Dream of Africa

ISBN: 978-1-988251-92-9

DEDICATION

To those who fought,
Those who died with a blissful thought
Those who derided servitude and dependence,
Architects of the Zambian independence
To you all, our venerate
These few poems I dedicate.

CONTENTS

CONTENTS

ACKNOWLEDGMENTS

I would like to thank my family for always being there for me: Clarice, Emmerance; Tashany-Idyllia; and Cuteravive.

The following distinguished and honorable Zambians deserve my acknowledgement, many of whom have given impetus to these poems through their comments and encouragements, in no particular or designation: Kalonde Chingwa; Robinson Kaleb Zulu; Chibamba Kanyama; Melvin Mbao; Lloyd Situkali; Kenneth K. Mwenda; Mutepuke Mwange; Tembo Boyd; Mwizenge S. Tembo; James Mwape; Victor Mwaba; Alisand Singogo; Khozi Sidney Makai; Khazila Chinsembu; Mushota Kabaso; Charles Kapungwe; Musonda Kapatamoyo; Musaba Chailunga; Viktor Mubili; and Munyonzwe Hamalengwa.

Others are Kasosa Mwinkeu; Hope Mwinkeu; Humphrey Mutiti ; Humphrey Salim; Elijah Sinyinza; Charles Chibwe; Misheck Nyendwa; Garth Chenda; Christine B. Phiri; Francis Boyd Brotherton; Marko Mulenga; Henry Chalishika; Ruth Kaluvi Sangambo Mela; Vivian Ngoma; Kristina Mubili; Sharon Musonda; Daniel Madiangi; Ali Kingston Mwila; Jacob PC Ntuntu; Timothy Ntuntu; Womba Nsabika; Margaret Mwewa; Coaches Musha; Sobby Kalebwe; Juma Mukonchi; Chris Tembo; Kwasila Nthaka; Andrew Shebby Zulu; Ackim Chirwa; and Ackim Katebe, to mention but a few.

Last but not least, Fernando Smith; thanks for penning a generous foreword to this book.

FOREWORD

In these moving poems on Zambia and Africa as a whole, we are presented with a vivid, compelling and masterful account of the realities of post-independence African life.

The picture that emerges from this poetic drama is a people destined to remove themselves from the clutches of colonial domination and in simple terms come to grips with their way of life.

Where did things go wrong for Africa in the past fifty years? What ingredients could have sailed the ship of Africa and Zambia in the right direction? What needs to be done for the benefit of the majority of the impoverished Zambians and Africans now and in the future?

Written by a Zambian intellectual and Professor of Legal Studies, this poetic landscape is both timely and informative. It provides as well some insights into how Africans live up to their cultures, including religious beliefs. The dance of their women and men while bare- breasted with their body movements to the rhythm and sounds of their forefathers is vividly portrayed as are all aspects of their lives.

African culture is one of its strengths and this is beautifully celebrated here. Sit down and take a flight.

Fernando Smith, B.A.
Co-author of Caribbean Best Seller
To Shoot Hard Labor

PREFACE

In 2011, I published *Zambia: Struggles of My People.* In this book I rather presciently predict the future of Zambia from what has gone before. I detail our struggles from pre-colonial days to colonial days to post-colonial days. It is documentation in time of the real struggles of the Zambian people.

It was barely three years after *Struggles of My People*, and as I look back, I was still touched by the quandary of my people. The year 2014 announced a Zambian Jubilee, 50 years of self-rule of self-determination and of freedom from colonial bondage from the former British Empire. It was on October 24th, 1964, when the *red-green-orange-black flag* was lifted and a new nation called Zambia was born. She was no longer a habitat of John Cecil Rhodes (Northern Rhodesia). The people of Zambia had become tired of being "boys" and wanted to be "men". Today, after 50 years of that so-called independence, we still are left with so many questions.

Foremost among these questions is: Are we better off 50+ years after the fact? It is clear that the answer or response to that cannot be fair, good or best. We may have to search deeply into our souls to be able to provide a better answer. But whatever route we may take, politically, economically or religiously, things have not been getting better. Some people might even say that things have worsened. However, such an indictment would be blatant disregard of the efforts and the progress the Zambian people, in particular, and some African states in general, have made.

Taking the case of Zambia as an example, successive Zambian governments have built some notable infrastructures in terms of schools, colleges or universities and hospitals. Most of these were built after independence. We may as well note that in terms of socio-political stability, Zambia – which in 2014 was ranked the third most peaceful nation in Africa and 44th in the world, according to the 2014 Global Peace Index and beaten only by Mauritius and Ghana – has been a successful story. Zambia can also boast of being a regional heavy weight in the way she has postured herself as a fountain of refuge and protection for all those running away from war, civil wars and regional distress.

Zambia has registered massive successes in the integration of tribal aggregates into a *One-Zambia One-Nation* formulation. This, in part, can be attributed to the spirit of compromise and tolerance our fore-fathers under the Kenneth Kaunda era tried and strived to impart at every level of government. In a way, it can be said that Zambia has recorded notable economic stability post-Structural Adjustment Program (SAP) era. This, though, is relative, and may not be accepted by all reasonable Zambians.

Politically, it is an elephant in the room, but speaking from an historical nuance, Zambia has done well in political changes after 1991. Kenneth Kaunda's undemocratic rule of 27 years cannot be justified even given the sometimes uncouth records of those who succeeded him (Frederick Chiluba; Levy Mwanawasa; Rupiah Banda; and Michael Sata, Edgar Lungu and Hakainde Hichilema).

Credit should, however, be given to Chiluba for ushering in the most coveted multi-party politics;

Mwanawasa for setting into place an agenda for economic progress; Banda for a short but frugal determination to hand over power peacefully to the Patriotic Front (PF) after failure to win the 2011 presidential elections; and Sata, despite his frail health, for showing that with courage a staunch Movement for Multi-party Democracy (MMD) government could be changed without resorting to the bullet; Lungu for navigating rather cautiously and with relative grace with regard to the issue of unprecedented presidential succession; and Hakainde Hichilema for his resilience and determination to win the presidency even after five (2006, 2008, 2011, 2015 and 2016) failed attempts.

In spite of the aforementioned and putting politicking aside, a genuine question to be answered is still this: Are we better off than we were before independence? We have done much to quell and curb repression and the rule of emergence regimes; we have instituted a working two-tenure presidential regime; and we have removed excesses in the quartered regime vis-à-vis our copper mining sector. But we still are tormented by the huge number of our people living in abject poverty, with hunger in rural areas, with lack or poor and inadequate education, and of course, our precious people dying from curable diseases. From whatever angle you look at it, and as I mentioned, politics aside, we have a long way to go to create conditions that favor a much more magnanimous and prosperous society. Zambia is still bleeding internally.

In earnest, I ask this question: Can we let this quagmire; this state of impoverishment follow us into the next 50 years? We have seen, we have heard, we have touched and we have felt, but it is time to *do*! And going by what has gone before, the current crop of the Zambian politicians may need to engineer new models and strategies. Even post-1991, they have not regained tract. They are old and tired, and if they are young, they cannot admit it, they have been made redundant by the ineffective policies and the 1970 economic models they still espouse, mostly engineered by the old frames of politicking.

Zambia needs renewed blood, new formulae and new assistants to drive the Zambian economic and political machines. We, the up and coming hope of Zambia, cannot insult the spirit and hard work that built our structures. No, we should not! We cannot ignore the good efforts the previous regimes have worked to instill. Even that, we should not! We cannot overlook the good intentions of those who died for the causes of our freedom and independence. That would be an error of historical proportions. But we should also not forget that if we sit and do nothing, we will end up with the same poor, stagnant and redundant results.

Where are the vibrant, the innovative, and our contemporary thinkers? Where are our educated lot, our exposed statesmen, and our assiduous intellectuals?

Where is the young, with their new and progressive ideas?

Where are the women, who still hold a key to Zambian, and African, progress?

Where are you, with your brain, your intellect, your time, your experience and your resourcefulness?

Where are we when Zambia, and Africa, needs us most?

Zambia, in particular, needs a progressive and golden thinker-brand. Zambia needs a new dream, a new hope, and a new perspective on how to run government and set priorities. If we don't want to change Zambia, no-one will change her for us.

In these pages, we sing, pantomime, dance and even frolic in anything and everything African. Because for a people such as us, with a vindictive past in our rear-view mirror, it is in order to do so to not repeat history. We have a land endowed by the Creator with everything that pleases the eye, is good for food, simulates the mind, invigorates reason, and deifies the soul. Because we have AFRICA.

cm

1 | I DREAM OF AFRICA

I dream of Africa, the smells of early rains
I long for the beaches heaving with swamps and fens;
I yearn for the dark long free worms, food for fishes
And I hunger for breams and all native dishes.

I miss the songs when new virgins' rites are over
With every step a rare chance to live in clover;
I wish to stand all day watching their curvatures,
As they emerge with tight chonches and fine cultures.

I long for your tender bosom, Oh, Africa,
I remember busking inside your bright Spica
As I milked in the zephyr of your youthful dawn,
And your *nshima* maize mixture I had always gnawn.

Oh, the rhythms of *rumba*, pleasure of your drum,
In this young, old, day and night, shindig and swam
To the sounds of mirth my ancestors bragged about
Oh, how soundly the children slept after the bout!

I often dream of the wastes lying on Cairo Road
Of graffiti and filth garbage across the board,
Of smut of compacted town-centre boulevards
Of uncouth conduct in courtrooms and churchyards.

I didn't enter the portal of the living dead
Nor tasted sweet love in a darkly flowing bed,
Yet, I dream of the best potential of all kids
Of women who dance with opened legs in all nudes.

I have been to the river banks of flowing blood,
To tears spilling over with a weeping flood;
In Africa they teach, "Life once given, it's gone."
Oh, land, without you it feels like I was not born.

These nights are memorable when I dream of you
These lights are horrible when I forget what you do;
These rights are fallible when I flout the offspring;
These fights are agreeable when I speak your feeling.

Some streets of raw Africa are littered with dirt,
Some central banks are warring with yawning debt;
Some roads are thwarted with problems of a pothole;
Some fields 've graves but music sounds make whole.

I stand at the edge of the rising waterfall
And watch able adventurers drive, dive and free-fall
On the waves of high splashing flurry and glory
Where they burry their heart and mind with no worry.

When I saw the smiling girls at their first instance,
When the bare-breasted ladies took their early chance,
Their thighs strong, their arms hardened through toil,
Their diamond hands, golden tongues drip silver oil.

The politics of the land are lovely as flute
The speeches of Parliament sound like awful fruit;
The decisions of courts are lithe like a Danseuse
And some banks lend only to those they can abuse.

The beauty of Africa is a fantasy,
Women keep their pubic gardens smartly fussy;
Men find it in parody of foreign accents
And presidents pride in signing stately assents.

The dreams of my homeland are many and intense,
The visions fill my beliefs with divine incense;
The fine blessings and the curse on the savannas
Are shaped like the anxious tendons near the anus.

I dream of your never changing magnificence,
In avant-gardism and now I see your presence.
Your vowel-ended surnames I love to pronounce
And your pure kind-heartedness I like to announce.

I hear the sounds of hip-hop filter through the air
I say, "Mwewa, to try the melody is right and fair"
For even though I grew up to the *rumba* number
Oh, I long for the sweet upsurge I can remember

I dream of Africa, I don't just exist as a number
In Africa, I have a talent, a habit, I am a member
In Africa, I have character and comportment
I remember, I am a dreamer but prescient

Like your people, Oh, Africa, your beauty is hidden
Until unwrapped, you remain under and trodden
But my heart cries for the places yet to be known
And here, listen to my song, my plea and my tone:

Perfection, to you is a garment
That fits my soul;
You're an epitome of beauty enfantile
And grace admixed in perfect measure;
Oh, this windily figure who moves hearts
With every step she moves heavens
And in every absence, oh my soul you crash;
Each day I live in the shadow of

Your fond remembrances;
Your heart, that fleshly gem in crimson,
Crafted from marble sinews,
Tender like angels' wings,
And lovely as a queen's chamber;
In your bosom mind and matter consent,
My untrained voice sings a song,
And my hands scribble lover's lines;
You stand as a mighty tower
And those legs taste like honey to behold,
To brag about your love is in order,
To say, "I feel you good" is bolder;
Oh, Heartcry, its poetry, lovely and true
Oh, Heartcry, like a woman, I love.

But Africa, forget not now thy bygone, depressive
And don't be silent to recount thy past, oppressive
If thou should dare to forget thy historical disgrace
Thou wouldn't care for thy future's glorious race!

My Africa is like a pretty woman without make-up
She wakes up in the morning with tea inside her cup
But neighbor's not happy; she's used only to coffee
She w'dn't give up her jerry-beans for brown toffee.

You are still a prisoner inside when you devalue race
But you are Nature's slave when another you duress
Africa, my love, learn to be who and what you are
For in the entire world, none gyrates softly like her.

Your ancestors will laugh in their graves at noon time
When they're told of what has become of your prime
Your muscles strong, big, you're about to be a man
But remember, O Africa, strength dies without a plan.

When you're all green and no poachers wonder about
When you're all smiles and the children do play out
Then we shall dance for the groom who has married
And our old, wise and accomplished we shall bury.

O Africa, my childhood lover, I love with every ounce
O "Land of Great Minds," be a hero just this once
O my dreams in the lands far away, in cold splendors,
O, how I long to be nearby your chubby meanders.

2 | NELSON MANDELA

I hear the news of the failing super icon, Madiba
From abroad, I see the rising rainbow over the Kariba
In my heart of minds, I offer him a fervent prayer
And from the heavens, his stars align in fresh air.

"Sleep in peace, great Star, in Qunu's ripe soil"
In South Africa, as in Africa, where we still toil
I was not by Africa's dust when you passed away
But a poem, "Qunu", to you I consecrate, and say:

The route to time-warmed freedom is still long
And is a thousand Mandela's resilient strong
The aura of the splendid Cape Mountains
Just lay few meters away from Qunu's fountains
For here, the great's remains have been buried
And here, his scepter of freedom's mantle is carried
In these terrains of bigoted Apartheid, he walked
And here, the towering figure of history has talked
To a people, but all the people of his homelands
For to one brother as to one sister all make bands
And here forever the light of the night has risen
In his long walk to freedom, injustice has fallen
Mourn all nations, if not this peace we butcher
For yours, not for the dead's, your new future!

Bye great guru, Africa's fortified soul in human form
Greet Nyerere and Nkrumah in their azure home
By-pass Mobutu and Abacha – say to them, "Shame;"
For these conspired to heighten colonialism's fame.

Let Africa in Mandela find a defence, a good name
For if what was done to him was also done to them
They would have said, "Africa is a brutal beast, evil"
But you forgave, and that deed, did shame the devil.

3 | ONLY US CAN CHANGE US

I remember a song I wrote, "Song of a Slave,"
I forgot to neither rhyme it nor recall to who I gave
But I will not suffer you to again resort to slavery
And never again, I sing, should they test our bravery:

A slave, a man, for that is what they have called him
From ancient civilization, the drums have beaten
And from the depth of the abyss, their gong have gone
Here, she was born a daughter from a man and wife
And there, they knew her as a fountain of calm waters

But for how long, the chants arise and the waves fall
And again, how long should we dance to nothing
As their progeny, we carry their humiliation, their pain
For in shame they bore mixed heritages, and for nothing
Oh, laugh aloud, our peril we chartered across oceans

How shall I sing when all nations frown upon the race
And as days old truths have been massacred in masses
So that when they needed booty, these ancestors died
So that when times of danger were done, they perished
But for them, these old lines will perpetually speak

In the name of God, haven't men flouted divine order
In the name of sacred scriptures, like dogs, they toiled
Even so they had them flogged with whips and strings
They considered them property, while quoting the Bible
For to them, they were nothing but personal chattel

Oh, cry sacrilegious, mourn, shame and hide your face
For now, pets receive more honor than they did
They were not humans, only expendable incendiaries
No vet would dare pock their noses; no justice found
Their women, their bodies they abused for wantonness

Should we dance, laugh or pretend all this did not be
Should we close our eyes to history as if we didn't see
Nay, for now and then, Africa is not a thing but dark?
And on the pillars of begotten statesmen be our mark?
Only endurance, only poesy, only us can change us!

We are "Not Just a Number" they make us to be
In movies, novels and stories, we are made to flee
Your land is turned into combat zone by politics
And old peers gave away your minerals to colonists

In this land of many 'chances and opportunities'
We still feel like we're numberless communities,
Nay, am not just a number, a color, or a race
Nay, I have a clan, a tribe, a culture, and a place

Again, I say, nay, I am not just a number on earth
For the medium is the peace, and strength in faith
Although the world panders like we're an event
And run to exclude us, nay, we are not misspent

And let them be a people, not a number, like one
These aren't just statistics, but hearts to be won
I dream of *Abantu*, Nilotes, the *Kwa* and the Sans
Daughters of the soil born to men who have sons

They say, "Africa is a land where fools carry wallets"
And "A land where the wisely-born hold mallets"
They also say, "Don't shape effigies and chisel wood"
But only, "Beg for a miser's penny for food."

It is wrong, it is wrong Africa when you they ridicule
It is wrong when they don't even come to your rescue
They're mistaken when they make a pyrrhic demand
I say, be strong, be courageous, and countermand:

There is nothing that may happen
That people will be hasty to say
That it was done without purpose
Since nothing happens for nothing

For everything, awful or lawful
Has an underlying meaning
This may not be now apparent
But will reveal itself in time

The law of life is take and give
So that in every circumstances
There is one gift that will offer
And its value grows when accepted

So, in whatever you are involved
Where your time and energy are
There is also your future and reward
And greatness in time it will award

Oh, City; tentacles it spreads like a pregnant octopus
Women in legs long and spacious coil, they freely pass
As down the busy and ness mesh, I walk, Toronto
How splendid your eateries, Africa, do come pronto

4 | NORTH AMERICA

In these north gardens, a superb summer sun shines
All the snowy dirt erosion brought to clashing lines
As the nimbus now grey canopy the silky skies
And here in northern whites the kite rarely flies

I see the scarlet macaw fly higher to gyrating rhythm
I think of the little rate that raced the plateau rim
Here the streets frolic in free pelting murky wintries
When the salmon, semblance to tilapia, finds entries

The greens, aroma littered from coffee plantations
Though none, from Ivory Coast's brown sanitations
In Canuck, seniors imbibe in what the land can't give
Yet, I miss the thick *munkoyo* gravy from our sieve

I hope for the western rainbow, which is color-blind
The East, people who are persons, their own kind
The South is not an island, it brags of a silver culture
Let the people merge, and kill that racial vulture

My people, all people, begin to make room
Do so to let the white-shadowed groom
With great diadem pass through to his fated doom
Where he'd be endeared into shape after one zoom

I say that the snake winds lazily in rush hour
They bumper as tolled-cars small and large cower
Where they're held up in the heat of burning oil
And here, their hearts curse the cost of free soil

I cannot say that I have totally left you, O Land
For there're days you weigh deeply on my mind
And, in Canada, I have planted seeds of amity
And here to the North Star I sing to fraternity:

The sun doeth shine steadily in Canuck
The flowers doth wave happily in Kanata
The grass in mountainless prairies
And cars through west speed to east
Spring doeth shine on caffeinated brains
Cows and bears in shades hide.

For you and to you, O Land of Africa, I write
Because like all poesy readers you have a right
So, I take a pen and cannot, just your face I kiss
And, these times of anguish, for it's you I miss:

I don't feel like writing poetry
For my darling Muse be asleep
To awake a drowsing mind
Takes more skill than rhyming
And the hand that draws and paints
Is saner than an idle clock

Oh, Africa, this love, that my wings be cast on sea
O Land, this love, the brightest in your eyes I see,
For in your hand melts love's melodies at best,
And every morning, I awoke to your palms' nest

Oh, Africa, you carry a heart of a true mother
O Land, and care for me more than several other,
Yet, you are only a silent lover of skins
When you're by my side, you're unlike other kins

Oh, Africa, I knew you'd carry me through the gravel
O Land, through Mibenge where we meant to travel
I see monkeys pelting freely in the tree branches
Whence Black Mambas strut in the golden trenches

I beg you, fatherland, I beg, Mother of mothers
Your good manners do not bless and curse others
For I was "Insulted in America" just for triviality
Those who despise you, thus, do praise banality:

They gather around media phones and shades
And insult me because I am not six feet tall.
They gossip of high art, music or movie trades
While me and others brave are left to fall.

They recite heroes in plots of love novels
And describe their figures of great beauty
But in all my experience and travels
I find perfection in a simple duty

My daughters say that Africa is handsome
And Europe knows Africa has great looks,
But the Americas have no sure ransom
And they dither to acclaim Africa in books.

In America they think all others are not good
They will say no-one from China and Japan is
They gang around basketball for their food
And wouldn't admit others can be fizz.

My dreams of Africa are many and have essence
There is never a day when I don't miss its presence
I see a democratic Africa, and a prosperous people
I adore you, Africa; I see the rising of a mighty hippo.

5 | ZAMBIA, I MISS

I miss home, the guiltless terrains of carving red sand
The waves of heated violet rays foment the land
Where in broad day-light, kids romp street to street
And with simplicity, the eve-drums, cheerfully beat

I am a character of two gene pools, I announce
I am unlike others, my last name I can pronounce
For he who can hear my accent, let him call my name
And here for you is a song, for glory and for fame:

Oh, my God, wow!
What wows is an owl
An owl lives in the trees
The trees grow in a forest
The forest in which birds hide
Hiding from slings and stones
Stones of lime and marbles
Marbles which built the city
The city is Ottawa
Ottawa is in Ontario
Ontario is a province
A province is in Canada
Canada is a country
Country is a genre of music
Music may be hip-hop
Hip-hop is an art
Art is made by brush and paint
Paint is of many colors
Colors may be in orange
Orange is a citrus fruit

Fruit may be sour or sweet
Sweet is like sugar
Sugar is from sugarcane
Sugarcane is grown in Brazil
Brazil won the 2002 World Cup
World Cup was in South Africa
South Africa is in Africa
Africa is a continent
A continent has nations
Nations may be Zambia
Zambia has 14 million people
People have different names
Names like John or Mwewa
Mwewa is in Bemba
Bemba is a tribe
A tribe consists of nationals
Nationals have races
Races may be white or black
Black absorbs light
Light comes from the sun
The sun is in the sky
The sky is in heaven
Heaven is, oh my God,
God's holy throne!

I mention Zambia, Lamba and Bemba in my dream
I fantasize about Kilimanjaro whence is my esteem
I love Caucasians, Blacks and all peoples of the East
And all races of nations from the North to the West.

I dream of *Insaaka*, where we collectively gathered
To the tales of our elders, for us, they fathered
We listened to oral traditions, rich and gracious
And now, here, their import I tell, simply precious:

For this tale
My father told,
This bird looks like
My own mother
Even the eyes look like
My own mother
The mouth looks like
My own mother
Even the ears look like
My own mother

Pounded groundnuts
Do you look like
Your mother or father?
For your mother is beautiful
Though you may look like
Your own father,
Resemble your mother
For she is beautiful

This stick is mine
I saw it at Katenta
This stick resembles my own
I got it at Katenta

This stick of mine has spots
This stick of mine has dots
This stick of mine is speckled
This stick of mine is
Black and white

This stick is dappled
Like a leopard
This stick is stippled
Like a tiger
This stick is freckled
Like a giraffe
This stick is speckled
Like a zebra

***

Nerves are cold, sullen and unexecuted
Energy is sour, squalid and inundated
Memory plays against views I inherit
All that is seen are souls without spirit

I miss the rhythm that skins ooze
Hear the sounds of tar-marked fuse
Speak with a waist and a hand is easy
And brace awake to untainted ecstasy

The music in Zambia is our brew
The sun showers with delightful blue
Shades dance and smug all day long
Flowers cheer to breezes fast and strong

Places are bumpy and chocolate brown
Mountains laugh with their chests drawn
Valleys whisper within spaces of native afros
In Zambia music speaks louder than it echoes

Unlike our fathers, we are not ashamed to brag
For we are inventors of our newly-scented rag
We make way for the Queen of *malimba* to lag
Whence they'll be followed by a boy carrying a bag

***

Oh, City of Livingstone let me a deep secret reveal
I miss you, but I have come to rediscover a veil
It is called Niagara Falls, sister to Mosi-oa-Tunya
But still, I cannot just forget your candid insignia:

City of Livingstone, Zambia
Many memories embedded here
In sands so loose and terrains so quiet
By Maramba, *sounds of shining colors*
The progeny of mixed races;
By Helen Britel, music glows to disco.
Here the route treks to Victoria Falls
The locals called "Smoke that Thunders" -
The waters boil at ephemeral speed
The environs warmed by rising fumes;
The monkeys sing to tangled thickets
Draining their natural call
On heads of state's bored-head!

City of Livingstone, Zambia
Canopy of Chief Mukuni
Who alone knows the riddle
Of Nyami-Nyami, a lady-snake
Who guards the river and waves!
Here civilizations meet nudely
On rapids, kayaks see-saw freely
Women under trees sit nakedly
While men watch so drily

The sun shines briskly at Sun Inn
Here lumpens meet their match
With sticks that sing, shoes that talk
Business takes on a twist
And a window to the future
Opens widely over Hillcrest skies
Semi broken; semi whole
So, we dingo to Kapentas partly rotten
To beans with skimmed insects
And meats that are cut like knives
City of Livingstone, Zambia
No place much better
No season much sweeter!

The dream of those who brought us independence
These toiled through speeches and correspondence
These are men of valor, resolve and nimble agenda
Some like Kapwepwe, Chona, Nkumbula and Kaunda

Though space would not allow me to call their names
I pay tribute to the blood that ended their life terms
To Banda, Chisembele, Lombe, Chiluba or Milner
And all others like Mwanawasa or even Arthur Wina

Yet, these dreams of the prescribed future still elude
Shall we dance after witnessing a damned prelude?
The life conditions deteriorate day, week or month by
For "Zambia I Cry," and in these lines I ask why:

The nation awakes to sounds of mourning
More frequently than it does to mirth
There is music in the air-waves burning
But not to celebration of life or to birth

Bana-Musonda just learned that her job
Will no longer be hers, but foreigners`
Children now run for help to the mob
And begging is part of the national anthem;

Small victories are displayed as mementos
A few malls are idolized as development
And education is a bygone word for ruiners
Inventions are rare and unknown for "them"
Talent is lamped to worst in churches or ghettoes
The nation feels like a chilling firmament
As workers and students alike resort to strikes
Since conditions are bad and the meal hikes
Who shall bring light to a nation in dark
Will the future be as it has been in the past
Are these leaders all look but on the back,
Oh, Zambia, O Land, stop sliding so fast.
O Land, you will no longer be an orphan
Your future is happy, your mêlée is won.

***

Learn thee to appreciate money, eat Native honey
And change thee thy warped attitudes on money
For thy errors regardeth economics make thee poor
And breedeth twisted facts of wealth for sure.

Know thee that money is existence's king
Understandeth freedom as the next of kin
As thousands lacketh its powerful thumb
In poverty countless doth daily succumb

Educate thyself in providence's drill
Coach thyself in how to pay the bill
For in hard times knowledge winneth
And in thy ignorance death ruineth

People ought to hold money in bounty
Every purse boometh with all that's plenty
And in thy plethora hold thee thy pass today
Do not stroll the earth amiss till Doomsday.

***

They may come from anywhere
In their path and from nowhere
The six messenger from hell
They arrive, they don't ring a bell

AIDS and EBOLA make their nest in Africa
CANCER lays her young in interior America
SARS leases her spores on seas in Asia
MERS rests her head in Eurasia

COVID-19, thou servest Africa of triage
And saveth mine land a purgatorial viage
But Europe and America thou treatest worse
Thus, forfeit hauling mine land in a hearse

Dig up mass graves in a desert
Deny Hitler a noon dessert
For all races as all colors, he refuses
Jews and Blacks he kills with gas fuses

No-one is innocent in Europe
None, when discriminations gallop
America pleads "not guilty" to blood
And Africa is submerged by a flood

I am not an author of tragedy
But I will not at all be rigid
I write what happens in reality
When so much lead to cruelty

I am not a critic of mass industry
And I will not keep my mouth dry
Nor do I see souls labor like machinery
Nor smelt stolen copper in the refinery.

I am for humanitarianism
Money is collected for many an ism
But in the poor name of the victims
While kids pair in miserable teams

I am not an opponent of aid
In the name of butter and bread,
I only tell of hypocrisy as a fact
Poverty and profit make a pact

***

In North America, I look back and miss zesty friends
In Africa, we played soccer and ignored petty fiends
In new lands, I write for consumer markets, edited,
In Africa, I'd pan it as, "Shakespeare Unedited":

For I, in mine dream saw Shakespeare
In the dead of night, I sold thee a spear
For the wife of that venerable Macbeth
This lady of vice and untimely birth
Thee, in thy dream, also saw Portia
In kind and mind as Obama's Sasha
Yet when thou awake did see thee Sinatra
The nard which played Cleopatra
Whence that night Julius Caesar
In battles trekked he with no visa
To surpass the spoils of Richmond
And to the Senate he gave diamond
Thou wrote on thy patch: Elizabethan
Which thou recanted to biblical Nathan
Who in predictions of David or Pharaoh
Who the priming looks of Romeo
Would dare not crown Richard the Third
Who did wear bloody gowns unaided
Who in the West careth for Africa?
What, but none singeth of Shaka.

6 | STRUGGLES OF MY PEOPLE

These lines now I write, shouldn't you read them
A "Tear of God" dries up on Mount Jerusalem
It is not for others, but for you, Africa, that I do pray
And these foreign corps, lie, but hear me when I say:

They lash junkets of donor support
On the pained daughters of the soil
All in the hope to redeem a race
Of a people mired in blood

The grim image of black Africa
Illuminated by an over-shined sun
Lamps its toxins of artificial gems
On a land deep in solstice shadows

This aid that always comes late
Given by greased governments
Is only a drop in a gigantean ocean?
As kids and women in tears bask

A tear of God lazily dropped
And who for Africa shall mourn
Who, for broken and forsaken land
Who, for stricken and afflicted brand?

Read my poem now I write, with tears in my eye
I title it, "Dying While Black" and I am not a spy
I try to understand the meaning of being Black,
Oh, Africa, it's not your name, for you're not dark:

They die brutal deaths, without a buck,
Just for being Black.
They are gathered in these prisons
Like chicken fused with deadly poison
They are readied for a mass slaughter,
A deep, dirty, Black smelter
Their only crime, their color
Just because of the skin's callow.

They lie in wait, these Blue policemen
And it pleases every serviceman.
These prisons are full of human sorrow
Creating waves with no tomorrow
When Black goes in saintly and dark
It comes out whitened, motives slack
When justice closes its eyes,
Law becomes a whip, equality dies.

The "Struggle of My People" are many, let me narrate
I write a thousand pages against the illiterate
Be not ashamed to be a member of the Black race
Because Africa is a better land, a wealthy place:

Alarms ring loudly deep down within long
We stand decorously secure and strong
Indeed, they enjoy life fewer peers have
They walk in streets structured with lights above

Haven't they the better of two worlds in one?
For our black beauties, hearts they have won,
Yet for our kids, I nightly toss bed's ends
I would not for a morsel damn knees' bends;

Nor for lack of pride shrink from your defence;
Nor at your poor's sight, create a Balaam fence.
Weary talents drain your brain, clan and blood;
In your precocious dead, doomed sorrows flood;

In lavish copp'r, hopes and stocks barely float,
Wryly, your faith rests in your ignored lot.
Freely, your limbs nimble in begging drills,
Drily, lax songs become your simmering pills;

Shyly, rules glue norms to lurid natures
Does poor peace frolic in vain adventures?
Morrow hides in shadows of green villages;
Mothers grieve in chants of brok'n elegies.

Zambia, loved like a mother who shaped me,
Cherished since I opened my eyes to see.
Our legacy, sign of freedom an' bondage,
Our past, a prayer of a shunned adage;

Let it be said that we had a thinking bard,
Let in books, your precious liberty bud,
Let in years to come it be said, "Ours knew"
Although in pride, grand, virtuosos are few;

Struggle is my people's fault-line of growth,
To freely prosp'r, is our true and bold oath.

O Africa, with dreams, you buffet me night and day
When I have said, "Surely I am free, I am faraway"
Even in that I am still tormented, I've not forgotten
The "Struggles of My People" signal me to return

Do not tell your child there is dignity in poverty
Those who have rights should own property
For me, I occasionally dream of the evils of lack
What I write now is real; I don't feel any black:

I wake, tears rolling, in deep sweats,
Dreaming of days gone with big debts,
In pain of worry and harsh nights
When sleep climbs over higher heights.

Dreams of poverty stir my soul,
I fear the day lack will befall
When gloom as a frightful shadow
Becomes a close and common foe.

I run from my footsteps all day,
All my plans have wondered at bay,
Poverty's shame does threaten me
And from my own heartbeats I flee.

The thoughts of days of want do haunt
The feelings of great need also taunt,
I see the pangs of struggle's past
I run far away very fast.

They struggle, yes, they have struggled since 1964
To gather food and spread a word of hope at four
Let the people rest from their hard labor for now
Let my people work less and enjoy milk from a cow.

The soul of Chiluba, the great Zambian flower
And the spirit of Mwanawasa, aura of power
And the placated horn of Mwansa Kapwepwe
Met to serenade Zambian hope near Kitwe.

In Zambia, in the years by and the flurries that shine
To Kaunda we learn the courage that is soft and fine
And we prayed for the good health of Michael Sata
For Rupiah Banda's contributions also to us matter.

These are our heroes, O the lion that be Nkumbula
We remember, we sing, O men and women of Ula
For he was Zambia's true advocate, O Mainza Chona
And may the tears that flood this land be our honor.

I dream of a land, I dream of your good times
No longer will governments be charged with crimes
I bring you an idea of "Change with Change"
When regimes go, people will have real change:

They claim they will bring change
When all they do is preach the old message
And their people don't find this strange;
You don't grow through the old passage.

People stare in mesmerizement and wonder
They have heard the same lies all their life
And they are confused and can't ponder;
They feel like they've been cut with a knife.

This Zambia I see shall from hence be *changed*
All hopelessness and hunger shall be challenged
My people will no longer be beggars in the street
But crime and grime, lack and muck we`ll defeat

My people have been worried about me going abroad
I blame you not, noble people, my reasons are broad
But this you must know, "I am not a fundamentalist"
And you I learn, for you I observe, and this is my gist:

I am not a Christian fundamentalist; I am a Christian,
There is a difference;
I believe in grace as Paul preached it to the Ephesians,
And I love the inference;
But there are those who use the Bible woefully amiss,
Such I avoid;
They pick this and for what does not, they dismiss,
That leaves a void;
God truly loves the world and does not exclude,
The good or the bad;
Yet, modern fundamentalists know whom to include,
And that is sad;
I don't use my faith as a weapon of condemnation,
I use it to help;
Everyone who is human fits into my combination,
And they don't yelp;
There is commonality in every extremity,
Christianity or Marxism;
Every act of love and care for the needy builds amity,
It mortifies separatism;
Embrace and accept all as composite brotherhood,
Which is veracious;
One world guided by one love and not hatred is good,
That is very precious.

Oh, cease, stop meanderings, stop accusing your past
You stop saying, "Why Me?" Archaism's long passed
You worry about disease, hunger and natural disasters
You endow them, blaming it all on colonial masters:

As I walk alone, along this busy street
Even in this silence on top of summer's heat
Thoughts torture my poor soul from within,
Frightful punches in my heart begin,
And I sob: "Why not me?"

I see those who live in elevated mansions,
Who drive elegantly and wear lurid blouses,
Who tint their cars and possess lots of money,
Who are followed by everyone like after honey.
And within me I glob: "Why without me?"

I watch men as they play on technology's best,
Women as they strut streets in angelic majesty,
I hear the winds blow at great force into aghast,
And all it leaves behind is me brownie and dusty.
In anger I ask: "Why not them?"

I am for all those who seem happy with life,
Who are accompanied by pomp so splendid
In their path they leave feasts of pride and strife
And have others wipe where they have fended.
With a banger I task: "Why only them?"

My people, to me you still glitter like the African sun
Early in the morning in your heated waves I am a son
Across the Crocodile River bed near Lake Bangweulu
To ancestors' blood libation poured, to our Holy Hill.

I see a green Africa, a fat and prosperous Zambia
I see a land with literacy, no hunger, no disease
I see a place of innovation, of technological bluffs
I see a clear tomorrow, of hope and peaceful bliss.

The simple things of the land of my birth
In your progress, O Zambia, still I hold faith
The sounds of song in the land invite me to live
With all I have and I am, I am willing to give.

The technology of my people is not simple as thought
In terrains harsh and conditions dry, even in draught
These sons, daughters work hard and early they go
These conquerors of nature deserve pride and more.

The vision of mice trapped in home-made *chiliba*
The fisheries along meandering streams on Kariba
How early we braved the early waves of the dew
And with spices and salt we dined here, too.

Don't laugh at the way I make my household, benign
In Zambia stomach pains aren't tendered by quinine
Windows of the town are guarded with burglar bars
My father's land is unsafe; my people are jilted by her.

And don't ask me to keep quiet, mealie prices are high
For a people who feed on maize and cassava thigh
I beg you, O rich corporations, do not shift rare millet
And do not replace *imbowa* with your blanched fillet.

Why do my people fear to work with hands, sorry
And how can we progress and tell a better story
My mother will sleep late tonight in the dark village
I cry, fill her path with fertilizer and light her visage.

There is hope frolicking sideways in the savannahs
And faith shouts from within the leaves of bananas
But love, for the land, for the weak, is desired much
This tyranny of many, our future it will not hatch.

The land where we share paths with fellow laborers
These dirty, brash politicians cannot be our deliverers
A media mogul is also like them, evil and ravenous
We spread democracy without being gluttonous.

7 | SAIL WITHOUT SHIP

Now I turn to you, Africa, and may they hear me
O Land, in your few years of independence I see
That you have been made to play host to secrecy
To shed your own blood for another's supremacy

Why should the West or the East still claim interests?
Why should they sponsor the political parties' trusts?
Why they aid war mercenaries and abet coups d'état?
Why – why change elected governments just like that?

Oh, Zambia, Oh, Africa, never step back on grace
Once you gave away your dignity, your first place
Why should a land so rich, so resourceful be third?
Even second you shan't, oh, give me your word!

My people say they are an independent state
When many of the citizens never sang, never ate
My people refuse to accept they are dependent
Oh, show me the budget; I see there is a dent

In my dream I see a band of thieves in government
These shady bosses, they will spare no moment
Oh, my people catch the crook, he who is corrupt
Oh, Land, never over-stretch the border, it'll erupt!

If I were a ruler, I'll ask for the US attitude
I'd set the missile, and I would fine the rude
I'd neither approve guilty nor free up treason
If I ruled, law would be above *all*, not a person.

O Africa, Oh, Zambia, night is too long for you
The honesty within you are becoming very few
But you excel in the art of forbearance, you do
Oh land of my fathers, without you, I'm who?

To "African Freedom Day" – the day I love to court
I was told it was like those released after being caught
But who says Africa was nabbed liked a silent gazelle
If that's so, Apartheid prisoners merited it as well?

We hear it so often at Remembrance Day in Europe
It anchors war memory like the cramp of a stirrup
Let America yell it loud, "9/11 – Lest We Forget"
Let Holocaust's clarion reel luridly as a floodgate.

All we like sheep led to its silent slaughter were sold
The brave, our ancestors, butcher-ed in liquids cold
Who spent miserable years in mephitic plantations –
Like putrid stench, were stripped on nude stations.

And Africa should say, lest we forget slavery's shame
Zambia, fail not to remember colonialism's blame
And if a people allow another people to oppress them
And they say nay, earth falls, in inglorious balm.

From coast to coast, the cash of your minerals shine
From open-pit to open-pit, dig ore to its core refine
Under the valleys of golden palaces where they mine
In riches 'n' wealth out of ten, you get yourself a nine.

The sword of injustice's blunted its sharpened edges
And to global security and amity we open new pages
Never to butcher each other again for light of skins
For in blood, we're all children of common of kins.

"Ignorance, Ignorance," call it just what it is
The wedding's cancelled, the bride doesn't realize this
For the sake of the young children, pray fervently
For the prosperity of the land, plant seeds reverently.

Let Zambia at fifty years old dance in the open places
The people say, "We hide all in the open spaces"
If the land exists as an island, we would clap and sing
But to tarry, we sleep; to beg is not in our gene being.

Stand and sing of Zambia, so our fathers declare
How shall we when 50 years still haunt us there
Proud and free we are, only if we puke out poverty
United we win, but at 50, is this land *our* property?

After 50+ years of civil independence, let us shout
After 50+ years, being another's slave should be out
After 50+, children in gen and wealth should thrive
After 50+, from curable maladies we should survive.

The politics of the land is empty in promises of gold
The tricks used all further the privileged and the old
The house is divided, pride flies out of the window
The young to poverty fall in a rising crescendo.

Oh, citizens, do tell your offspring in the night watch
And you brethren, why did you distinguish the torch
The tremors of post-independence tsunami break out
"Independence from Dependence" is what it's about.

Do sing, my beloved, shout it out with great joy
The mighty within you have not fallen, it is a ploy
They invented the Millennium Goals not in vain
For NEPAD is a byword, so are coups with pain.

There is something in Africanism, *ours* is a country
If the young are trained to think, they display gallantry
The makers of social systems and slogans 'r' dreamers
And social media isn't for desirers of costly creamers

We have traded in useless warranties, mourn my lover
We offered sacrilegiously on altars with ancient cover
We started, and did not finish, and another is credited
How long, how long, beloved, will you be unmerited?

African Renaissance is a conspiracy we've dreaded
We've never faded, no, not once, we've been raided
Now we rise and speak, Oh, my land, don't be quiet
For your intellect you've not shown them quite.

For once, let us see you for who you're, gorgeous
Stand tall, flex your muscles, you're courageous
For long, you've worn gowns made from abroad
Stop it, craft elegant garb from your inroad.

Shall we say that we have the name of fame to affirm?
We shudder under the blunder we can't confirm
We hide beneath the canopy of "Black", Oh, Africa
We are Africans; pride it and we ride in A-Free-Car.

The daughters of my Motherland are very beautiful
Against the Fatherland, they pretend to be unfruitful
They paint their lips and color their curved hair
Africa, as a bride I love, you've always been so fair.

You are not blind, Mother, see for yourself, see all
You were not raised as an orphan, please feed more
And let no-one tell you what to do, you have a *brain*
If you keep us within your laps, there'll be no *drain*.

You are not deaf, Mother, even when you keep silent
In your eyes, I can see plainly that you are innocent
At your heart, you accommodate all, great and small
And in your mouth, grace and peace dutifully flow.

Let us now beat the drums and prepare to dance hard
Let us make a banjo, a marimba and call upon a bard
Let us shake the waist poignantly till the heavens fall
Let us now sing, "Mother who bears us is for us all."

8 | PROMISE ME

"It's time to do something," stand, do a thing
Hitherto, these leaders have said everything
The people for years have waited for nothing
Yes, for the people of Zambia, do anything!

Do shine, shine river of flowing copper cathodes
Educate your young, refine with myriad methods
Though sea access is nil, rain spouts are wide open
"Seed & Job" will sprout, and *growth* will happen.

Mother Zambia, that is what I call you, O Mother
But you`re more than a mom, you`re my Father
In your soil my ancestors buried their birth codes
And I sing, here to you only, as I do the land nods:

Mother...
Of mound display
An unexplored Eden in Africa;
Full of Nature's best
And an endless of tradition...
(To Zambezi -
To pay an invocative visit:
The people on superstitious gravity)
To you Mother...
Higher vows I pay.
Your soils are veins of life,
The peace
The joy
The resting
Your people, my people,

Occupied
In structures of thatch
And decorated mad walls!
Your idyllic terrains;
Much more unexploited.
Your virile bushes;
Much less inhabited.
Your smiling hopeful visage
Is the ink that pens this message…

***

My country is a Christian nation,
A declaration of the century
A transition indeed
To the people in need.

My country is a Christian nation,
A declaration of good faith
A transition indeed
To a people who read.

My country is a Christian nation,
A declaration of trust
A transition indeed
To a people who hate greed.

My country is a Christian nation,
A declaration of divine Providence
A transition indeed
To a people great in deed.

My country is a Christian nation
A declaration of goodwill and grace
A transition indeed
To a people who in love will breed

My country is a Christian nation
A declaration of political hegemony
A transition indeed
To a people who've been freed.

***

They fought as a band of soldiers;
They died while fighting, as martyrs,
Some are forgotten if they lived,
And others have scars to show for.

We meet them daily in grey hairs
These are our truest statesmen,
These our prized gallant fighters,
Pillars on which we live and thrive.

We their brood their glory will save
Never to forget the blood they shed,
And in their footsteps we will follow,
Attesting to hearts strong and brave.

This freedom so for granted we take
With sword and pain was achieved,
Even when many in pieces returned,
Silently, yet very clearly, they speak.

In libraries their heroism archived,
In pain and anguish they travailed,
These sons of liberty are of renown,
Heroes of peace, our true veterans.

***

Passing by Chitambo we saw a tomb
Whose epitaph was a dual petition
To the god of the feast of Hecatomb,
Written below was a re-petition.

He passed away with hands in akimbo
After braving the nip of fillaria,
And shunning many calls from the limbo
But was met by a shell of malaria.

This man bemoaned a German war Gotha
And found a panacea in helpful Chuma
Whom he taught the secrets of Golgotha
Whose blood-flow cures the tumor of Guma.

We hear sounds rattle from clouds in Congo
Sending dark and heavy rains of defiance
Smashing civilizations as ingle,
Washing them out without any reliance.

We come home back to village Chitambo
To water the plants of our great Sambo
Whom we rhyme in our book about poetics
Who savours the Zambian politics.

Africa is now a Cinderella
Her beauty should not be spurned as loveless
And a reed-mat shouldn't be her umbrella
And she shouldn't hold poison, gloveless.

***

The vile wars of Banguanaland:
Let me lament for the beloved
And compose a dirge to her plot.
My beloved has a spacious land
Sited between two great waters
Of Indian and Atlantic seas.

She dug it up and cleared out stones
And planted therein dire landmines;
She built a loom and secured it.
She dug around mass shallow graves.
Expecting to bring on power,
But alas, it brought gushing blood.

Dear kindred of civilized worlds
From Cape to Freetown, to Khartoum,
From London to New York and passed:
Did you observe the kid soldiers
Who are forced to drink human blood
And are strained to eat human fresh?

Wambo is factory to limbs;
My beloved's air is polluted
With gases of ruinous rockets.
Which countries make all fighter jets?
In whose interest are they shaped?
And who fashion weapons en mass?

Wars fought on my beloved's top soil
Have tainted its fertility
And rendered its earth impotent.
They die unceremoniously
And are buried without prayer
An offence to God, their Creator.

Refugee camps stripe my beloved
Just like the skin of a leopard
And the world believes it is free
Poverty, like locusts, invades,
Ballots are nothing but a ruse
While laws only favor the rich.

The nations fob watch from a mile
And monitor as man kills man
Think it will never haunt them!
People in Banguanaland bawl:
Guiltless children worriedly howl,
But do you hear their hopeless roar?

***

At the tip of Africa,
What hilarity and grandeur!
The temperate west coasts
Of the lovely eastern grooves,
The sea, the rivers and oceans,
All together weave
Into a lovely impression.

The land of light and beauty;
You have come to South Africa,
The people in carefree moods
In houses panelled and lofty
By black and blue labors.

You hear the sounds of cars
And see the noises they create:
The best places are here
Where life goes to the brim
In the heart of Johannesburg,
The world's city.

Here are buried in rands, gold
And its display
In splendorous Eaton centre.
South Africa, absence of Apartheid
Is a-free-country,
A continent at the tip of Africa.

***

In the area of Luapula
The nut-growing marsh of Mansa
Drums loudly beat on scapula,
Whence flat bums are but cancer!

She is just a small tender girl
You can count her black pubic hair
Her chest empty like a funnel
While her nipples are red and bare.

She prods on Bangueulu plateaux
With silly gazelle-like blushes;
She only prefers troupes of twos
With virgin peers in the bushes.

The rare wisdom of her betters
Has not yet charmed her frail figure;
She is shy through her dried fetters
And her lips are out and bigger.

She is not a woman, per say
Her blood is still cold and impure
Because the full moon is far away
To chaste her fresh and to endure.

She has not danced Infunkutu,
The arrangement of three drums,
The ancient rhythm from Timbuktu;
Nor won the dry skins of wild rams.

She will be taught *akalela*
To learn how to open taut legs
And she will know *amalela*
To make foetus from fertilized eggs.

They will soak her in Munwa stream
To broaden her pelvis
And fulfil her childhood dream;
To break the curse of a novice.

The sweet juice of soundless rivers
Elongates her wombly shaft
To cure every natural fevers
And purge the lucky winner's haft.

Her sully frame will be made firm
Decked with Kolwe's pure diadems
To date, she has well-run her term
And will earn the prize of rare gems.

Outside, she is cramped with shivers;
Her life's canal is perfected
And her full pulse proudly quivers;
But her *self* is unaffected.

Her body is bottle in form,
Her nipples are now hard and full,
Her buttocks are firm and uniform
And her waist is mellow to pull.

She has been accepted by Ra
Goddess of the erect solar,
And the shining fruit goes to her,
To court gods of the other polar.

She's joined the Aushi women's core
Who cause charcoal to burn brightly
And make impotent nobles whole,
To mix blood and water, rightly.

She can now handle Mandingo,
The killer of angry male lions,
That dancer of the hailed tango
Who with just bare hands breaks irons!

Prefer we the Aushi women
With their ever-protruding backs
Which confuse sanity in men
And accord night the force it lacks.

Their place in humanity
Loses its share in virility,
Gains it in masculinity
And modes it in fertility.

She kills the eyes of on-lookers
And she is not for press showings.
Suitors treasure her like vodkas
And her heart beats higher than wings.

Do not expose her publicly;
Her nude was made for great virtues.
They pass-out rather too quickly;
Those who resist, become statues.

A love son of Luapula soil
Has never known to marry two.
Legend has it that he will toil
And his garden, he will not do.

Oh, these Luapula Aushi curves,
How succulent their deep bosom,
In which mankind vibrates life's waves
And men's desires bloom and blossom!

Sing to her gyrating shifts
And swing through her softly paired rifts.
Mark nimbly her alluring nod
And make safe love in fleshly gold.

The open fields of the lake side;
Here breams bread simply and early
Elders gather to placate size;
And approve dancers of the belly.

Oh, our Luapula, Luapula;
Land in which babies grow fuller.
Where mothers nurse with open breasts;
And men's hope in the night rests.

In here perfidy is punished,
But fidelity is ever prized,
Impotence is overtly banished
Yet, all children are greatly priced!

From Luapula, let us build bridges
To cross Zambia through the rough ridges
For the woman is our anchor
And in her womb, is our banker.

***

To you my darling mother,
My one and only
And I don't have another.
My dear family
Has entreated me not to
Ignore history
And our own origins, too.
This is our story
I tell in tears and sorrow
And it offends us
Deep into our bone marrow
After as soon as

They notice that we are black
And color doesn't cheat,
They also think our blood is dark.
We may take the heat,
But we have been strong
To speak to the face
That all along they are wrong
Since we know that race
Speaks volume of variety
And none is superior
Or all-wise in entirety
To think inferior
Of others who are diverse
When reason is in reverse
That today's culture
Is mixed civilization
Of a past nature and wherein
Is Africa's immunization.
Sing you in skins black and dark
For legacy is the braves' mark.

***

This Zambia I see will cease to be led by paupers
The land will be cured of all toxic grasshoppers
For they who rule for gain will be eliminated;
Put first the *governed*, and you will be serenaded

This Zambia I see will vim with vivacious vassals
The fervor of *vox populi* will enliven state vessels;
Vixens will be victimized, the vigilant will thrive
But civil vultures will vanish, the brave will drive

This Zambia I see will be a land full of plenty
The people will live above fifty up to seventy
The dreamer will dream, and so will the visionary
For many will also do the work of a missionary

This Zambia *we* see is for all, *all* have like rights
There no longer shall be internal political fights
None shall be snobbish; all shall be free to think,
Plan, play and pray, *work* and break, and to drink

Stormy though the ride may be, or dark the night
Fly, in red stained sacrifice, green and golden bright
Under this flag, Black is home, no more in serfdom
At Anthem's clarion, able we are, at last freedom!

Arise, O Land, wake up, O noble people
This is not time to hook loads to the nipple
It's time; it's time to do, not to resign
You golden generation, come out and shine

Zambia, I, a zealous zealot with a zest for zitherns
Zapping to Zambezi in zigzag a zillionth zains
Zealfully I zone and zoutch for thee, O zee Zed
Zit not Zoë, but all zombies, zax from zero to zed

Zambia, how lovely the *mukwa* doors of Parliament
Zambia, when it passes laws in hurry and merriment
Zambia, how beautiful a true people's government
Zambia, when citizens' wellbeing is its disbursement

Bear witness to Zambia Thy chosen, O God on high
Not golden-pride or war maketh great, but Thee nigh
Bless this land, with Thy bounty and unmerited grace
This Thy nation protect, Thy peace be in this place.

9 | STRONG AND FREE

O Africa, I have loved you with pure love
Like an eagle flying up and far in the above
So beats my heart, for the memories of you
O Africa, compared to many, there are a few

You have been my lover, my keeper, my anchor
You secured my undone frame in your banker
And now I remember your infinite loving-kindness
And your unfading and unbridled goodness.

From the lands of the White people, I recount
I look at your history from which fortune I count
That at the beginning of your journey to far here
You kept our promise, "For you, I will be there!"

O Africa, land of unfiltered and sober music
In manners and etiquette, O Africa, you're basic
But the dance of your people my soul it reaps
And your rhythms, a dagger rips mat my heaps.

O Africa, your face never leaves my brown visage
I wait for you, my sense glued to your long image
For blood and tears have run through your soil
The rule of fear has threatened our flowing oil.

I will love you always, O Africa, I will not forget
Your anthem of peace and freedom is my fete
I will never cease to remind you of true loveliness
Of that unadulterated African neighborly selfless

In your brown terrain lies the hope of the earth
In your unplowed villas there I will put my faith
For the children run freely in the early morning
The elegy is no longer our song of mourning.

Africa, should I call you a champion of the sufferer
Or the captain of those who hold the Emperor?
In the art forgiveness, you excel like a frugal god
In endurance, you stand the test like purest gold.

***

I am a proud African,
Let the drums beat, the forest shake, the rivers flow
I am a proud African
There is an eternal blood in me, vigorous and steady
I am a proud African
From the lands flowing with gold and diamonds,
lands of my ancestors
I am a proud African
I have built civilizations, toiled for nothing and
reaped the wind
I am a proud African
Others mistake me for a bigot, a slave, a thinkless brat
I am a proud African
I have birthed inventions, and my name is not
associated with any
I am a proud African
I am strong, daring, fearless, and my veins drip with
ripped marrows
I am a proud African
My wisdom is in my color – dark, black and fits with
any variance
I am a proud African

I am the hope of the world, I still treasure the jungle
filled with greens
I am a proud African
My shape is a bottle, I treasure the rhythms of my
protruding buttocks
I am a proud African
I speak with divine accents, feed with the roles of
nature and sleep free
I am a proud African
This is who I am, I don't want to be another, nor
serve another
I am a proud African
I love all, never discriminated, never enslaved another
race, I am pure
I am a proud African
Generosity is my outer wear, and forgiveness is my
inner garment
I am a proud African,
Abused, but never retaliated, cheated but never
repatriated
I am a proud African
Others think that I am dull, unsophisticated and
clearly brainless
I am a proud African
Tolerance is in my DNA, the past eluded me but the
future is mine.

***

Oh, Africa, at the tip of the Old Benguanaland,
The land of the Zulus and the Xhosas,
Therein Shaka of the Zulu brought us pride,
Thy gyrateth like none other,
Thou danceth as the goddesses in Brenda Facie,

Or that angel only known as Malope!
In terrains where Mandela's gongs clearly gluing,
O Africa, south of the continent,
Thou art our blazer.
In that 2010 atmosphere,
Thou hostedth the Great Cup
To the sounds of Beautiful Shakira
And rhythm of Waka-Waka!
Or "This Time for Africa" –
Oh, Mother Africa,
Mother of mothers, I honor thee!
From the land of wintry whites and polar bears,
Surely, here in Kanuk's maple groves,
I remember the tropics in their thickets,
Surely, Africa thou art gorgeous, land of my fathers.
Oh, South Africa, be a land of soccer's grandest
dribblers,
I surmise, time is now to dribble thine troubles.
And thee, Africa, be to me a trophy,
A garland of victory.
It's time for Africa,
Thou heardeth me, a faint voice from Zambesia
It's time for Africa,
And may the waves of grace to thee,
An orison from our Heavenly Father be.

***

Oh, Africa, my Africa,
Don't you amaze me
In all wise, you're poor
And sometimes even evil
Other times, you disappoint,
Especially when children you neglect

Your roads are full of potholes,
Some of your housing dilapidated
You keep enjoying other nations things
And you don't pay attention to your own potential
You spend more time copying other people
Than you do trying to improve yourself
But I still love you
I am dead in your rhythms,
Especially your Rhumba
Your girls are lovely –
As soft as the feathers of a peacock
Your music – oh my God –
I can indulge in day and night
And your beauty – is true beauty –
The nature, the people
Oh, Africa, although you're neglected,
My thoughts are all you
Africa, my Africa, no matter what,
Our love is forever
Africa, till I die, we are two roads that met
And have promised never to part
Oh, Africa, my Africa, God shine upon you.

***

Africa, never sell our pride laughing
Never again, sacrifice our children bluffing
Africa, never accept a barrel of a gun
Yet, again fight to free all, economic, again.

Colonialism is not of civilization
It is a crime, its anti-Zambianization
Should we stop, it should be smashed
For all unfair history, it is be stashed.

Africa, sell not thy nudity for pounds
Pride not, but gym to lose more pounds
Thy fat, thick lips and dark ebony are fair
And fairer still than bleach, dye not thy hair.

You aren't a victim, end the impasse
Build your own factory and campus
Say, "I am but original, I am culturēd,"
Guard your names, lest they be butcherēd.

O cry beloved when nations fail to know
Thy blood isn't a black river of harmful gall
Thy huts are built with skill and creativity
Free thy mind, indeed, of all alien cap'ivity.

The standards are set, Oh, don't imitate
No, be yourself, faking will irritate
Your children are completely whole
Crave no light skin, no, redeem your soul.

Know, study and deep greatly into history
Explicate all angles, and get the true story
Africa, blackness is not equal to dullness;
Far be it from truth, neither more nor less.

Zambia, books forsake not, math ace
Africa, educate thyself, redeem thy race
Zambia, let thy genius be seen by many
Africa, till thy land, shy not from any.

Africa, be home to all on Mother Earth
The great keep, science and more re-birth
O Land, many secrets thou hast kept
Do sentry thy edge, cease from being inept.

My people, vile things have been done
You've not lifted your voice; you've gone
Struggle, again and again, again and again;
Plough thee this land, for soon it shall rain.

***

Oh, give thanks, give thanks to God Omniscient,
The One who is all things, and most sufficient.
In Africa long ago, they knew You as the Omega,
Indeed, in vernacular, this rhymed with mega.

Although they had no history of Christianity,
They were not at all devoid of sensible humanity.
They observed Nature, in it they discovered You;
In their customs, it was clearly You they knew.

They could be enchanted by how You made them,
They had no doubt it was from You they did stem.
They could be amazed at the meandering of rivers,
But they believed that it was only You who delivers.

They were astounded at the heights of mounds,
But they heard Your voice in surging sounds.
In all these, they never stopped to be thankful;
They knew You're immeasurable, You're tankful.

They played drums, flutes and pipes for their God,
They didn't tire to follow, the Protector of Old.
They were flabbergasted by unusual life events;
With libations, they flooded You with presents.

They know You in their mother tongue as Lesa –
And in many dialects, Oh, God, You are Leza.
You're Africa's, You bless her soil, Oh, Nzambi;
You have achieved ascendancy, Oh, Kyumbi.

You're Bore-Bore, kids sing of You, O Mongu.
You're famously known as Yala, Asis, and Mungu.
In dry season, You supply food, O Kalungu
The skies are full of Your splendor, O Mulungu.

You're big, the biggest, You're called Mukuru.
You busk in Your eternal glory, Unkulunkulu.
You bring the rains and winds, O Ukulunkulu.
You'll rise for Your people, Chindi-Chaimana.

You laid the foundation of the world, Kiibumba,
And beautifully designed its borders, Kabumba.
You unleash Leviathan and slay the Black Mamba,
For You're known as the Dragon Slayer, Pamba.

Oh, Most Venerate, You're honored as Yatta.
You're the Great Father, in Bemba, You are Tata,
And by all, worshipped as Zanahary and as Chiuta;
You are Almighty, You roar, Oh, Lion of Judah.

You reign in an unapproachable glory, Nyame,
You have revealed Yourself as Leader, Nyambe;
You display Yourself as Olodumare and Ondo,
For You are the Self-Existing One, Oh, Olo.

Oh, Lord God, You rule over kings, O Inkosi,
For as King of kings, You're Inkosi-yama-Nkosi.
You fight battles, and the bounty is theirs, O Tilo
You're worthy to be followed, Oh, Adunbalo.

And who is like unto You, Oh, Lord Mwari?
Surely their ancestors loved You, as they do, Ori;
From eternity, You've been merciful, Great Wari,
For Yours is the power, the praise and the glory.

You are decorated, Mighty Warrior, Oh, Rugaga,
You are the lifter of Your people, Oh, Olugbega.
You return triumphantly, O Lord, Great Hero,
And those who hate You, will inherit but zero.

Almighty God, You give all things, Oh, Ruhanga
You drew them in Your palms, Creative Chilenga
For You know the end from the start, Kalunga,
Your love, has not deserted Your lovely Africa.

You're victorious, glorious, Almighty Modimo,
You're meritorious in deeds, increasing ever more.
All nations of the earth look to You, Oh, Urezwha
And Your goodness is shared by all, Osanobua.

You are, and can be, many things – You're Oluwa
You do and undo anything, Almighty God Ruwa;
You justify the innocent and the humble, O Suku;
You forgive sins and show endless grace, Chuku.

Khuzwane, to describe You, there're no words,
Imana, because You are affected by no swords;
You are the true God and Lord, the Invisible One,
You're the way, truth, life and victory You've won.

A diversity of people knew You simply as BIG,
For in You all promises, pledges will never renege,
Oh, blessed be Africa, Your land of amazing hope,
Of her, You've spoken in prose, verse and trope.

You've graced Yours with stamina, Great Njinyi,
In their dire need, You've'nt forgotten them, Ngai.
You're their King, Sovereign, their Great Oba;
In Africa, You're like a Mother, *the* loving Baba.

10 | KENNETH KAUNDA

I heard about your timely death from abroad;
You fared well, now respite in the blessings of God.

At the time, I wasn't able to attend your funeral;
You're rested by the scepter of fewer a general:

Where Chiluba, the giant of multipartyism, is buried
Where Mwanawasa's fight against poverty is carried,

Where Sata's allergies for corruption are unvaried
Where Banda, Lungu and Hichilema's 'll be ferried.

I wonder if they broke your coffin, laid you in reeds
And surrounded your regal head with Mwalule beads,

As the elders did make a deal in Kapwepwe's pride,
Whom they quickly honored, wrapped in a cowhide.

I wanted to be among the mourners of an Africa giant
Who against Apartheid's evils stood boldly defiant.

I hope they wrapped a white kerchief on a wreath;
You preached peace, turning green an African heath.

You dreamed of a united, one country, one nation
You fought colonialism, HIV during your duration.

You harbored Mandela, Machel and freedom fighters;
You're named among pioneer presidents and writers.

During your life time, you advocated for refugees,
You ate vegetables, had fewer wrinkles and noogies.

A proud nation's father, you were, and for it you died;
In your footstool, we will follow, with shoulders wide.

Even though a one-party stands as an arrogant effigy,
 That tainted part of your legacy and our self identity -

We are grateful, however, for your militant courage
Against regional civil wars which you did disparage.

Let me your notable life serenade in works of poetry,
And put closure, "Saying Yes," as to a song by floetry.

You're right, you would live forever in our memories;
Which we'll hung on walls as memento tapestries.

11 | AFRICA, GUN OF ECSTASY

Oh, Africa, my Africa
To your blends of sumptuous foods
Your generous land of glorious goods
Oh, Africa, my Africa.

The oceans that surround thee
The brilliance of the dolphins
Induce a jiving melody in me
Thy fishes, glow in biting fins.

The smile on your striking girls
Oh, Africa, beautiful thou art thy
In darkly mouths white teeth swirls
In these hairs, boredom waves bye-bye.

Nature, Mother Nature,
You have been children's nest
In pure drinks, your virtues do nurture
And to Africa, your most is our rest.

O, cradle of world civilization
Africa, home to a people with a mast
Your pension neglected to desolation
You're rising, O Land, forget not the past.

Your sunsets, God has blessed thee
The trees and plants dance in the eve
All curses on the fringe do flee
O rejoice, Freeland, it's no time to grieve.

Hail Africa, your cultures shine like the sun
Hail Africa, you stand out among many
Hail Africa, all impurities shalt be shun
Hail, Mother Africa, grace you have plenty.

Oh, roar, roar Africa with a din of glory
Shout in glorious jubilation, shame insecurity
Oh, narrate your foregone tale in a fairy story
Your magnificent waterfalls embody surety.

Oh, carry me, sure Africa, carry me
At the junction of serendipity
Let me meet the honey-making bee;
Embrace me for the sake of our privity.

Wow, wow thy offspring in thy famed azure
Do deck them in spacious brooding skies
And drive us in modern pride to our sature
Whence thy vicissitudes thy nature defies.

Thou shaped world genius into shape, Africa
In the rising Sphinx, loves meet sensuality,
Thou chiseled the edges of blub'ed America
And broughteth frozen mirage into actuality.

The pride of your plateaux are rare routes
To the epicenter of pleasure drive calmly;
Break not, spare not, lead straight via thy roots,
Stand thee bravely, flavor thy culture's assembly.

Africa, you are a gun of ecstasy, a weapon of
pleasure
Thy l-shaped borders hive with havens of pure
treasure
From thy eastern barrel to southern tip, cometh a
bullet of love;
Thy western trigger, issues amity from thy grip north
above

ABOUT THE AUTHOR

Charles Mwewa (LLB; BA. Education; BA. Legal Studies; Cert. Law; DIBM; LLM Cand.*), a prisoner of grace,* is a Dad, author, lawyer, educator, and moral and social influencer. Mwewa is the author of 35 books and counting in all genres – fiction (novels), non-fiction and poetry. Mwewa, his wife, and their three girls, reside in the Capital City of Ottawa, Canada.

INDEX

D